Seeking the Light

— POETRY FOR THE SOUL —

VOLUME 3

Ana Lisa de Jong

LANG
BOOK PUBLISHING

LANG
BOOK PUBLISHING

langbookpublishing.com

National Library of New Zealand Cataloguing-in-Publication Data

Lang Book Publishing Limited 2016

ISBN 978-0-9941419-6-5 – Paperback
ISBN 978-0-9941419-5-8 – Hard Cover
eISBN 978-0-9941419-7-2 – ePub

Published in New Zealand
A catalogue record for this book is available from the National Library of New Zealand.
Kei te pātengi raraunga o Te Puna Mātauranga o Aotearoa te whakarārangi o tēnei pukapuka.

WHAT OTHERS ARE SAYING

'*Seeking the Light is a perfect benediction for
Ana Lisa's Poetry for the Soul series. Like her
earlier books, this overflows with inspiration.
Ana Lisa is incredibly talented and gifted. Spirit inspired,
she is able to translate her emotions and feeling into
such beautiful and engaging verse. I like her honesty.
Many of her works echo both the joys and struggles of
her life and faith, so masterly captured and conveyed.
Her journey becomes our journey as we relate and
empathise with these poems soaked in feeling. Seeking
the Light not only captures the essence of Ana Lisa's life
and faith, but also inspires and illuminates the reader.*'

CHAPLAIN CLASS 2 COLIN MASON,
PRINCIPAL CHAPLAIN DOMESTIC SERVICES
NEW ZEALAND DEFENCE FORCE

'*Seeking the Light, by Ana Lisa de Jong, holds a strong
sense of anticipation. Such is the spirit of seeking. This
third volume is 'food for the soul'. Seeking, sharing, waiting,
reflecting, trusting, following and holding on are key to
the process of seeking the light. God, who is the 'Light
of the World', desires to shine through the darkness.
Here is poetry that brings a calming effect
when calamity may prevail.*

"*the still pool*"
"*the reflecting image*"
"*I am he who both makes you and will keep you*"
"*the Light still seeks me out*"

"I see you, seeing me living light"
These all are words that speak of security,
sensitivity, sufficiency and sincerity.
Buy it, read it, share it – the whole 38 poems.
PETER SAVAGE
CHAPLAIN COMMANDANT
NEW ZEALAND DEFENCE FORCE

'*Words flow from our hearts and from our souls. The rhythm*
of poetry nourishes and renews us. Ana Lisa's poetry is a
delightful and refreshing expression of this. Her words minister
to my spirit and my soul, bringing healing and rest.

As she comments: Faith is the healing power of light and the
illumination of our pathway ahead and her words provide
that healing and illumination. A wonderful collection to
take on a retreat or to use as a daily devotional focus.'
CHRISTINE SINE, CO-DIRECTOR
MUSTARD SEED ASSOCIATES/GODSPACE
GODSPACE-MSA.COM

'If life with Christ is a journey, a pilgrimage from temporary, inadequate quarters to our glorious, eternal home, the poetry of Ana Lisa de Jong is surely a cool, clear stream that runs beside the pathway for a ways—a place of refreshment where weary travellers may kick off their dusty shoes and, dangling their feet in the cleansing current, simply rest.

Here the spirit is bound up, the words on the page reaching deep down to draw out the pain of loss and labour. The soul is encouraged to rest in quietness and to regain the strength that once it knew; the heart with its memories of past hurts and sorrows is gently washed in the love of a God who wouldn't think of allowing us to travel in the dark without light.

As I turn the pages, again and again I wonder at the uncanny way in which the words bring to mind feelings and hurts that even I didn't know were still lurking there in the shadows. This is going to take longer than a simple afternoon rest by the side of the stream. I may have to stretch my hammock between two shade trees and stay here awhile.

But, Ana Lisa's words again remind me that life is indeed, a journey. And, journeys require traveling, not putting down roots. Even though the way may be dark, there is always "a way forward". Our Guide sometimes "sees fit to shine his light only where he leads." No matter. In faith, we walk with Him.'

PAUL PHILLIPS
WRITER/BLOGGER
HESTAKENLEAVE.COM

'There is a crack in everything;
that's how the light gets in.'

LEONARD COHEN,
SELECTED POEMS, 1956-1968

Words

Words.

Words drip from my heart, to my fingers,
creating art, in written form.

Words.

Shining gems, of water, to be held,
and written down,
before they've run out, and dissolved.

And the words

always surprise.
As I, silent witness, watch my feelings
take on substance in my mind.

And become words,
from which meaning is derived.

But Words

words, like art,
are never quite adequate, to express the artist's true imagination.

And so words

become something like a mirror,
conveying the reflection of an image.
Not the whole truth,

though close enough.

But the words.
The words, they flow still,
not limited by how exactly I can decipher their meanings.

They just come, the words, like rain.
Which I grasp, and try and impart, again and again.

Knowing their power is in the feeling,
not the translation.

ANA LISA DE JONG

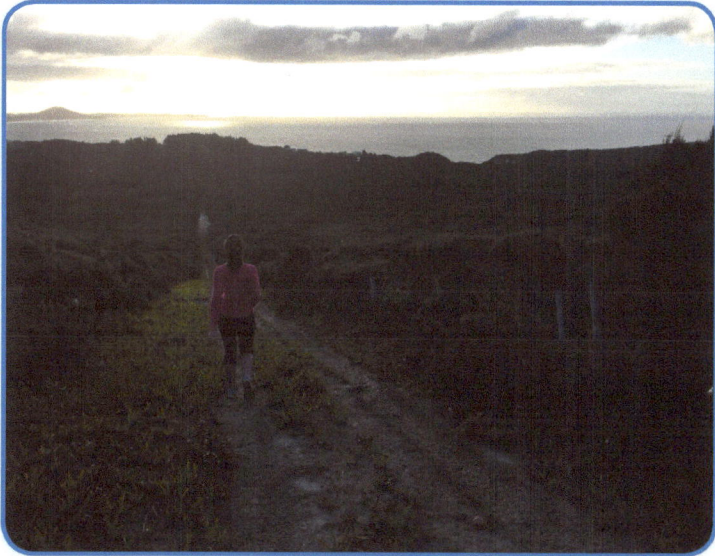

'The world is full of poetry –
the air is living with its spirit;
and the waves dance to the music of its melodies,
and sparkle in its brightness.'

FROM 'POEMS', BY JAMES G PERCIVAL

Contents

Foreword

Only someone who has plunged into the depths of life's story may rise up again with stories to share about light greater than any darkness experienced. Ana Lisa brings each poem from the depths of her heart to you, the reader, as personal gifts of grace. Each poem may be lingered over with the healing presence of the Father, carried like balsam in these pages.

Lines rise up with revelation, touching places within as though they were written for you alone. Yet, they rise up to encompass our greater story, as children 'seeking the light' and finding it in often surprising places. This is the third volume in Ana Lisa's 'Poetry for the Soul' series and brings the series to completion, with the ripe abundance of summer's blessing. Each poem is a friend waiting to be encountered.

No matter where you find yourself in life's journey, these poems, accompanied by beautiful photography, will bring you closer to the love of God for you in unconditional proportions. As you read each one, a window is opened into contemplative prayer and the presence of the Holy Spirit. You are met, face to face, with hope and wonder. As you linger over this volume, you will find poetry to deeply connect you with your Heavenly Father, and poetry to read and to share with others who need to hear for themselves, that there is a future hope and that light is always there, pursuing each one of us.

The timing for this volume of poetry is now. Never before has the world needed such healing presence. Now is the time for seeking the light. Now is the time for sharing this light with every heart that needs to see once again that 'the light shines in the darkness and the darkness can never extinguish it.' (John 1:5)

With a feeling of great honour I write this Foreword, knowing that you, as the blessed reader, are about to be deeply met. Go forward in the knowledge of the ever present invitation into light that reaches into all places. Seek, and you will find.

Jenneth Graser

Poet/Writer and Author of *'Chasing the Light: A Devotional'*

secretplacedevotion.weebly.com

Introduction

As this new volume of poetry came together I considered its theme and realised that it was a story about light. How light is always present. Even in the dark night, there is light from the moon and the stars. Light enters the crevices of our wounds and the cracks of our facades.

Light illuminates our understanding. Sending a beacon of hope into our future and shedding a balm of grace upon our past. Light continually rises in our hearts, as continually as the dawn of the new day. Even the seed in the dark ground holds the memory of light, and knows what to do in order to reach it.

Where is light there is hope and confidence. We think that light is revealing, so we hide from the exposure, but if we let ourselves be found, we find that light is not harsh and unkind but gentle and transformative. Light speaks of new days and brighter seasons. Colouring our future with promise, and healing our past.

All three poetry volumes of the 'Poetry in the Soul' series, including this volume 'Seeking the Light', point us towards God, in his son Jesus Christ, the author and finisher of our faith. Faith could be considered another word for light. Faith and light give us eyes to see. Eyes to see ourselves in a surprisingly gentle light, reflected in the eyes of our creator. Faith is the memory of light (the seed in the ground) and the expectation of light (the new day dawning).

Faith is the healing power of light and the illumination of our pathway ahead. God's light is not a harsh, man-made flourescent beam, rather it is the light of the slowly rising dawn, or the sliver of silver-lined cloud in a stormy sky; it's the traces of light through drawn curtains, and patterns of sunlight on floorboards; the sudden warmth on our skin as the sun breaks through cloud cover, the warming rays of a winter fire or solitary candle.

God's light is gentle, welcome and benign; but relentless, especially when our own darkness threatens to overwhelm us. His light feeds our faith; faith in him, in each other, in ourselves. This faith grows in us to reach all the darkest corners of our beings, bit by bit, and we find in time that the light of faith that floods our hearts, feels a lot like love.

Ana Lisa de Jong
Living Tree Poetry
June 2016

'You, Lord keep my lamp burning;
my God turns my darkness into light.'
PSALM 18:28 (NIV)

Walking Home

We are all walking home.
Such a long walk.
In the light, and in the dark.
Sometimes hand in hand,
and sometimes alone.
Sometimes, we stride forward
steady on the path.
Other times we trip on the stones,
on the verge.

In the day we can clearly see our way.
His smile, our light.
We know his hand of blessing,
and his gentle guidance.
While at night we feel our way,
and struggle with what we thought we knew
so well;
what had seemed clear to us in the light of day.
We encounter ourselves.

We are all walking home.
And light and shade define our days;
just as sun and moon distinguish
day from night.
If there were no questions or regrets;
struggles, slips
or back-tracks,
then we would have arrived.
We have not arrived.

Yet we may look, and find,
the blessing in the night.
Those things we cannot see in the daytime,
have a way of surfacing in the dark.
And without our eyes to see,
we feel instead, their edge.
And realise again, our deep need for him,
who, although we cannot see him near,
keeps vigil by our side.

'For we live by faith, not by sight.'
2 CORINTHIANS 5:7 (NIV)

Wait

We wait.

We wait for the evening's respite, for the week's end, for the spring to come, again.
We wait for the weather to clear, for the sun to shine, for the days to lengthen.

We wait to take a break, we wait for opportunity, we wait for time to do, all we've been planning.
We wait for blossoms to bud on the burgeoning wood, for the leaves to green, and the bird's dawn chorus.

We wait for health, and wholeness, for full healing to come and revive our spirits.
We wait for inspiration and words of discernment, and a sense of God's clear calling.

We wait because we know

there's better around the corner. That love grows, and time heals, and joy comes in the morning. Which is true, but it is also true too, that God, our God waits with patience, 'to be gracious to us' too.

He waits.

While we wait for the tide to turn, and the river to subside,
and the leaves to change.
He waits at the river ford where we make our own way,
challenges the stepping stones.

He waits while he has us, moulding to his hand's shape,
in the heat of his kiln.
He waits while we thirst in the wilderness, patience
doing its perfect work.

He waits for our yearning to cease, and for us to recognise
the blessing in every heartbeat.
As the acorn is split open, in the moment life is found.
Not ahead and not behind.

So he waits.

While we wait for summer to come, for seasons to change,
and his favour to return.
He would that we would hear him calling in the moments we discard,
wring out life for all its worth.

As he waits in the here and now.

'Yet the Lord longs to be gracious to you; therefore
he will rise up to show you compassion.
For the Lord is a God of justice. Blessed
are all who wait for him!'
ISAIAH 13:18 (NIV)

The Silver Lining

There's a silver lining
waiting to be seen,
by the eye that can perceive

purpose; and if not purpose, meaning.
And if not meaning,
then at least,

a gift.

That might look just
a little different,
to what we were wanting.

Hard to recognise,
and to become accustomed,
but always, always

what we need.

It's just we never know
what we need,
until it comes to us,

in forms we didn't expect.
But if we look, if we look,
we find what it was that we needed

by what we get.

Perhaps silver linings are
treasure, greater than the
fulfilment of our small intents.

Their value lies in their
sneaking up, and
catching us unaware.

Leading us to reassess,
the true purpose here.

'Lord, I know that people's lives are not their own;
it is not for them to direct their steps.'
JEREMIAH 10:23 (NIV)

Back

Go back.
Not to stay there.
But to find, what you left behind.
What remained undone, and follows now at your heels,
waiting your return.
What goodbyes were not said, or griefs unexpressed,
on those back steps, or the long ago hospital bed?
What was left?

What has you now,
going round in circles?
Looking, longing, looking, longing,
for you know not what?
And what bandage have you applied,
to distance yourself from past regret?
What mask do you hold so tight, in the fear it will slip?
What wounds, with a knock, tend to split?

Go back.
The words that were never said.
The hopes dashed, and expectations unmet.
Be brave enough to acknowledge the needs
that still remain.
From what you couldn't help;
or could have helped maybe,
but believe yourself
to have failed.

Write.
Write away the pain.
Find a friend and speak of the ache.
Speak until the words finally dissipate.
Speak to those whose faces are long gone.
For their presence lingers, till you do,
in every pattern you repeat,
and stronghold which has you bound.

I'm going back.
Not to stay there.
But to re-track my journey up to now.
Until its clear where it broke,
and cracked.
And where I made the replacement,
thinking I had mended
the ache of loss.

Oh how wrong I was.
I'm coming back.

'He will wipe every tear from their eyes.
There will be no more death or mourning, or crying or pain,
for the old order of things has passed away.'
REVELATION 21:4 (NIV)

Understanding

I must make sense.
I need to make sense,
of the feelings, which without their unveiling,
might drown me in their midst.
If I didn't draw them out,
hold them to the light,
see the beginning from the end,
understand.

If I did not investigate,
address the darkness
and call it by its name,
then the darkness would enfold me,
and despair steal all the gain.
All the treasures the darkness brings,
not revealed by day,
would go unclaimed.

So I must make sense.
As my heart beats
to a tune I'm yet deciphering,
I must listen to the beat,
to what makes it tick.
Take up my pen, and translate.
Knowing that, though these feelings might resist,
I must explain.

'Blessed are those who find wisdom,
those who gain understanding.'
PROVERBS 3:13 (NIV)

Fooling Ourselves

We fool ourselves.
Believe ourselves to be attached fast
to the leaf.
But shaking in the wind,
as blossoms on the branch;
buffeted enough,
we find ourselves,
airborne.

We fool ourselves.
That it won't be our turn.
Comforting others,
measuring out
our careful wisdom;
we forget there will be a day,
we will need,
our own medicine.

But we all have our days,
in the sun,
when we blossom, and bloom.
While the days in the wind,
we resist and turn from;
though they come
unrelenting,
to everyone.

So I fool myself.
Believe myself secure,
and steadfast.
Living tree, roots deep in the ground.
And I am: deeply rooted,
and aware of my source.
Yet the wind, with a life of its own,
still abounds.

But what if I said 'come'?
'Come wind, what may.
Lift my blossoms, torn off my limbs,
give them breath, and uplift.
Show them the view
from up high.
Show them there's more ahead,
than what I can see, right now.'

'And that my security,
my security lies not,
in holding on, till my petals are damp,
and torn.
But in letting go,
in finding freedom in the uncertainty,
trusting in the life source
of all things.'

'Show me, Lord, my life's end, and the number of my days;
let me know how fleeting my life is.
You have made my days a mere handbreadth;
the span of my years is as nothing before you.
Everyone is but a breath, even those who seem secure.'
PSALM 39:4-5 (NIV)

The Night Watchman

'I will wait, I will wait up with you.
I will wait until
the soil is dry,
of the tears that have fallen,
until the sun crests the hill
and the new day is dawning.

'I will sit with you in the garden.
If you are awake, I will be too.
I will not slumber while there is
hunger in your soul,
I will stay while
the night lingers still.

'I will keep you company
when the loneliness bears you far
from the presence of others
who cannot follow.
Who cannot know the things
that keep you up at night,

those things which you feel alone.'

'But for me. But for me, who comprehends.
Who understands,
what it is to sit and to grieve,
without the comforts of a friend.
To feel the shadows bearing down
on a cold and barren ground.

'Yes, I am the one who has been there before,
the dark night of the soul.
And because of this
you know, that only love for you
led me to the garden's floor.
And its love for you that moves me still.

'So I will wait, I will wait up with you now.
I will wait until
the fear subsides, and
the light that seeks you out,
starts dawning in your heart.
Yes I will wait with you in the dark and lonely night.

And you will rise with me in the light.'

'My soul is overwhelmed with sorrow to the point of death.
Stay here and keep watch with me."
Going a little farther, he fell with his
face to the ground and prayed,
"My Father, if it is possible, may this cup be taken
from me. Yet not as I will, but as you will."
Then he returned to his disciples and found them sleeping.
"Couldn't you men keep watch with me
for one hour?" he asked Peter.'

MATTHEW 26:28-40 (NIV)

As With Love

Time

moves on, while we wish
we could hold it still.
Expand it to retrieve each precious morsel.

But nothing still holds its worth.
Its value in the passing,
and the measuring of its gift.

Held in freeze frame,
it would only stagnate and shrink.
A still pool reflecting little light.

Its lack of breadth,
closing in on itself,
until its eventual demise.

So instead

we let it pass.

Yet, if we look carefully
beyond our apparent loss,
we may see we're richer

for the moments invested.
The memories enlarging us,
to contain more to take with us.

Yes time moves on,
and we wish, how we wish,
we could halt it.

But time like love
has one true common denominator.
It endures beyond us.

And as with love,
which we only keep by offering up;
so with time, we draw treasure from what we relinquish.

'For this world in its present form, is passing away.'
1 CORINTHIANS 7:31 (NIV)

An Ending

Lord, the sun has shone in brilliant blue.
But today, the clouds skim across a sky of every shade, and mood.
I listen to the wind, strong in the trees, and hear myself say,
'Thank you God for all seasons.
Thank you for beginnings, and for endings.'

The sun comes and goes.
So do smiles, and caresses and moments.
Everything was designed to change and end.
We are fools to think we can stall what's always moving,
or remain exempt from life's evolving.

Thank you God that all we touch somehow we keep.
Despite it changing tomorrow to something else.
Just as the sun burnishes our skin to golden,
so memories mark our hearts and enrich our souls.
They ground us and define us, as we move on.

Though the flowers we picked yesterday no longer bloom,
there are more to find.

'There is a time for everything,
and a season for every activity under the heavens.'
ECCLESIASTES 3:1 (NIV)

Trust Him

Ask yourself.

What direction do you want to take?
Smooth as water,
which knows its way;
or fighting the current
for wasted gain?

Let go.

Don't hold on tight.
God's river runs wide, and carries us all.
His blessings kept safe,
and his purpose sure,
in his river of deep shalom.

Abide.

Don't fight the tide.
Surrender to the waves that come.
Dive deep, to where the world grows dim.
It's there you find your pathway clear,
gleaming as the sun.

Follow him.

Believe he knows what is good.
He draws the ocean by the moon.
How much more has he determined,
your small affairs,
of great worth to him.

Trust him.

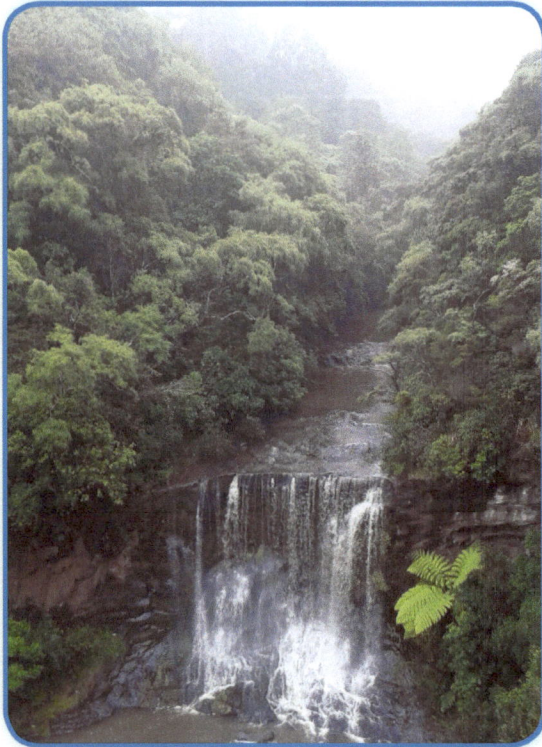

'For in the day of trouble he will keep me safe in his dwelling;
he will hide me in the shelter of his sacred tent
and set me high upon a rock.'
PSALM 27:5 (NIV)

Let Go

Let go.

All things have to be let go,
released back to their source.
We can only receive a moment.

For as an embrace, a smile, a glance
were never made to be retained;
so we hold briefly in our hands, our gifts.
Drink deep from their blessings.
Thank God,
then cast them away.

'Forget the former things; do not dwell on the past.
See, I am doing a new thing...'
ISAIAH 43:18-19 (NIV)

I Love

'I love',
I hear myself utter.
I love - what?
What is it that I want?
Something beyond
the extent of my grasp.
That other,
that goes undefined,
and unharnessed.
The unknown that I
believe might
satisfy all my longings.
What is it,
which without, I suffer?
And get caught
in incoming desire.

'I love'.
Though I know
there's no help for it,
I still want, and love,
exactly what?
And If I had
what I longed for,
would that be enough?
Unlikely,
for as the tide, briefly in,
runs back out;

so our needs,
have their moments of release,
before they then renew themselves
once more.

'I love'.
But love is not about
our wants,
or their relief.
Unless we love beyond ourselves
it's really only emptiness
that we are trying to fill.
And with what?
Just more of the
insubstantial.
No love,
in the end
must be its own offering;
must turn back in upon itself,
and love, love again,
what is missing.

'I love those who love me,
and those who seek me find me.'
PROVERBS 8:17 (NIV)

Seal Me

Seal me in your heart.
Seal me in your heart oh
lover of my soul.

Prise me open to you,
and to you alone;
because your love for me
is to the death,
and your jealousy,
strong as fire.

My only answer
to such a love,
is to fall upon my knees.
Captivated by a love
that will not let me go,
pledged fast to me.

And all that you ask,
in return,
is that you are my one desire.
Above all, who may draw me
from your feet,
above all the world's allure.

Oh seal me fast,
tied to your side,
for I'm inclined to wander.

Though I know there's no-one
who can touch the spirit,
beyond heart and soul.

But for you.
But for you, my God.
My love, my desire, my all.

'Seal me in your heart with permanent betrothal,
for love is strong as death, and jealousy is as cruel as Sheol.
It flashes fire, the very flame of Jehovah.
Many waters cannot quench the flame of
love, neither can the floods drown it.
If a man tried to buy it with everything
he owned, he couldn't do it.'
SONG OF SOLOMON 8:6-8 (NIV)

Self Compassion

Should we not give ourselves,
that which we would not fail
to feel for another?
Compassion.
Understanding.
Willingness to suffer,
alongside.

So sit with your sorrowing self.
Hold your own shaking hand.
Feel the strength that you
can impart, from one palm
to the other.
Lift yourself,
strong again.

We were all born
sensitive, and vulnerable.
Though we may profess
self-assurance,
we still need the gift
of a non-judgemental self,
to serve as our sturdy backbone.

So let yourself be honest.
Sit in the midst of pain.
Listen as you might to a friend
to what your heart
is not saying;
but might, if it had the courage,
to follow its unravelling.

You are strong.
Though born in weakness,
and dependence,
your will to survive
whatever you were thrown,
is ingrained.
You are still the same.

Though we may feel alone,
in our deepest self,
we need not be there unassisted;
and without the grace,
which self-compassion,
in its hope and love,
will always give us.

So trust yourself.
Encourage the foot which
stumbles behind.
Your sensitive heart in
its softness, and strength,
is the re-builder,
of all that is broken.

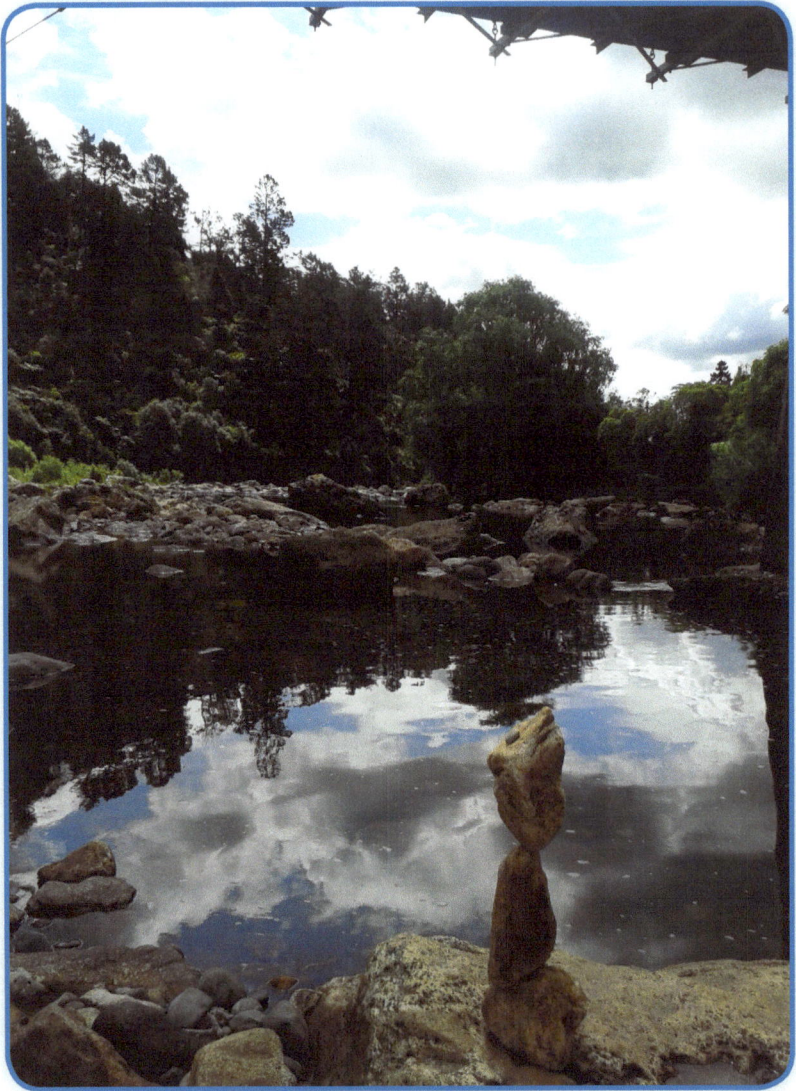

'I call as my heart grows faint,
lead me to the rock that is higher than I.'
PSALM 61:2 (NIV)

Silence

'Amazing grace,
how sweet the sound.'

But 'grace' -
what is its sound?
For as I bite my lips
a thousand times,
to stop my sharp retorts
rebounding,
I realise grace
is more often found
in silence,
than in words
which resound.

More often found
in restraint,
than words
which state my case,
that I might be justified.
Yes, words to express God's heart
through me, must subside,
must give way
to listening,
hearing, reflecting
on another's deepest silence.

Words,
if they must be said at all,
must come from the depths
of stillness inside,
where truth and grace meet.
Where my message is refined,
until it is worth more
than what I might express in silence.
Until then grace,
if it is true,
is quiet.

'Your people will rebuild the ancient ruins
and will raise up the age-old foundations;
you will be called Repairer of Broken Walls,
Restorer of Streets with Dwellings.'
ISAIAH 58:12 (NIV)

Rest

Rest is an echo
that finds us again,
when we've shouted too far
into the void,
when we've tried to scramble
up cliffs that deny us a foot-hold.

Then rest is an echo,
that speaks with your voice.
Reminding us that
it is pointless to strive,
without your anointing,
and your peace.

For though we know
we have your aid,
you remind us that we're
not to work without taking breath;
without making space,
for your voice, amid the noise and haste.

Among the vestiges,
of all we've sought today to achieve,
all we've sought to be, for other's sake,
as well as ourselves;
we hear you in the disquiet
of our muddled thoughts.

We hear you in the echo,
and know that,
all that truly matters, is what you've asked of us.
Which is never, never more
than what we can handle right now,
in this very moment.

And rest, which we think of as so fleeting,
is actually our inheritance.
And you, who reside at our centre,
are our peace and shelter,
that surpasses all understanding.
The voice which fills and empowers us.

'So is my word that goes out from my mouth:
It will not return to me empty,
but will accomplish what I desire and achieve
the purpose for which I sent it.'
ISAIAH 55:11 (NIV)

My Little Flower

'My little flower.
I see you when you're unseen.
I see each breath of wind,
on your petals.
Know each passing breeze
that moves across
your foliage;
as though it were my own
hand touched, and
touching your skin.
Each reaction, of yours,
felt and known,
in heaven.

'My little flower.
No sunbeam falls
on your leaves,
or rain buffets your form,
without my protecting shadow
overseeing my creation,
ensuring your provision.
Take heart.
Nothing passes past me,
without my knowledge,
nothing touches you
without my
first feeling its impression.

'You, my flower
see the rain, sun and wind,
as servants;
to which, for your growth,
you are dependent.
See me in the storm and
in the quiet after,
and the solace of the night.
Your roots will only grow
to the depth the wind shakes
your branches;
and the extent the elements
strip the earth of nourishment.

'For my little flower.
I am the deep living water
in the underground reservoirs,
made to carry you through
each season.
I am your sustenance,
despite the leanness
of your circumstances.
I am he who both made you,
and will keep you.
In the storm, the stillness,
and the sunbeams,
you are tended.

'And the infinitely worthy object
of all my attentions.'

'Through him all things were made;
without him nothing was made that has been made.'
JOHN 1:3 (NIV)

Loved

Loved I am.
By a man.
Who knows me.
From inside out,
not outside in.
Who understands.

Loved.
And never alone.
Though I may believe I am.
Until in the stillness
I recall, my heart's
held in his hands.

I could not be alone,
if I tried.
If I had wanted to live
independently of him,
he would draw me yet
to respond to him.

With a lover's relentless
pursuit.
Loved and cherished
beyond measure.
Held
above all comparison.

And what could I do to be unworthy,
of such love?
Nothing.
Safety, security.
In the knowledge of
his tender presence within.

Yes loved, I am.
By a man.
Who knows me.
From inside out,
not outside in.
Who fills me as others cannot.
And whose every touch
is kind.

'I have loved you with an everlasting love.'
JEREMIAH 31:3 (NIV)

Love is Not

Love is not love that grasps.
We love large enough to let go.
Anything less is not love.
Maybe love for self, but not the other.

Love that is large believes.
Upholds the other's dreams.
And swallows the loss down whole,
so the pain is kept from leaking.

Love is not love that grasps,
but bravely holds its smile.
Fighting the urge to secure,
the things that can't be held.

*'Dear children, let us not love with words or speech
but with actions and in truth.'*
1 JOHN 3:18 (NIV)

His Light

It is a way forward,
this light, however dim.
And even if I can see my way
only one step at a time,
I trust in the guide
who sees fit to shine
his light only where he leads.

And though I pray
for so much more
than what I can see
by his light right now;
I must trust
what he yet hides from me,
as much as what he reveals.

Because he promises.
He promises, that though I doubt
I can yet believe;
can trust in a future
still dimly perceived,
through the misty veil
of hopes and dreams.

I can depend on the fruition
of his promises,
and plans, though they may differ
from all I've yet imagined.
They are designed to fit our frames
and not to chaff and hurt
as something ill-planned.

Yes, it's a way forward,
this light, however dim.
And what matters more,
is not what's held in store,
but the truth, that he accompanies
his children on their journeying,

and we're to forsake our crowns, for his.

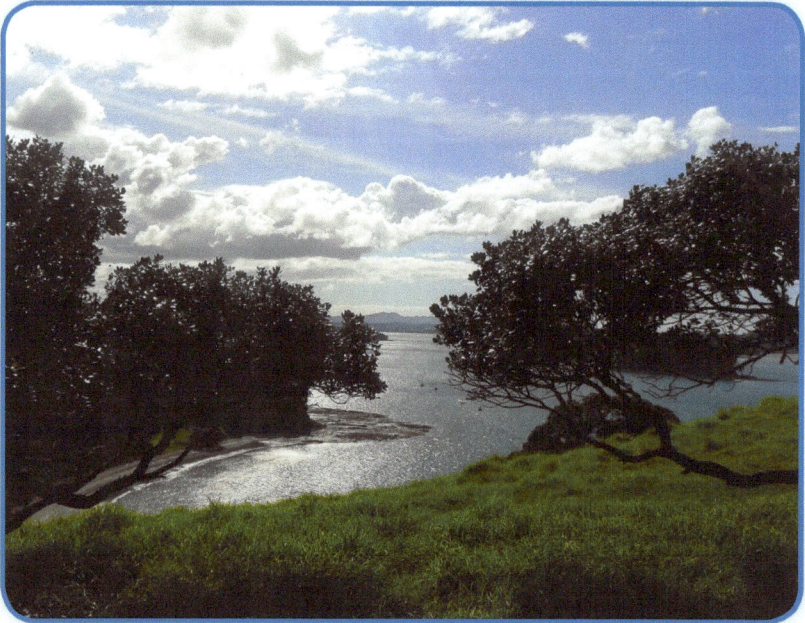

'…And the light of heaven will shine
upon the road ahead of you.'
JOB 22:28 (NIV)

Cocooned

Looks deceive, dead seed pods
and limbs bereft of leaves.
Grey leaden sky,
and chilling winter breeze.

We hunker down,
layered like the earth beneath.
Wondering what still lives,
what might still breathe.

But looks, they deceive.
For under the pile of cast-off broken leaves,
as quiet as the tomb,
the earth holds its breath.

And waits. Just as we awake,
breathe and stretch towards the light,
so the earth waits,
still, and expectant of life.

Yes looks deceive,
for underneath, stirring and lengthening,
are seeds, growing to bursting;
awaiting the turning seasons.

We too are mistaken,
to believe nothing is happening;
brittle hearts covered,

in last year's debris and bracken.

Wondering how renewal and restoration,
can appear a possibility,
when all is sodden?
But lo behold, life is coming.

Like sun on snow,
our hearts begin thawing.
Like light on the hills,
spring ascends the horizon.

Not one moment too soon, nor too late,
in arriving.

'Sow righteousness for yourselves, reap the fruit of unfailing love,
and break up your unplowed ground;
for it is time to seek the Lord,
until he comes and showers his righteousness on you.'

HOSEA 10:12 (NIV)

Come

Come home to yourself.
Home is sand under your feet,
and sun glinting silver on the sea.
Home is the waves and the birds,
warmth on your skin.
The solitude that brings you home,
to your soul.
Forgo the crowd, which leaves you lonely,
and come away for a while.

Come back to yourself,
survey the view.
And you'll remember,
that you've never been away.
Just been wearing something ill-fitting,
waiting for the day you can disrobe.
And run barefoot.
Dishevelled, wind in your hair,
but free.

Come take a walk.
To the hill where the sky is large.
See the evening spread like a curtain across the day.
And feel yourself small, but wide.
If you still yourself you will hear,
your heart beat along with the earth's.
And you will know yourself a part of the whole.
No separation at all.
A particle of life.

Which can seem lonely, unless you recall that,
your footprints leave a mark on the sand.
You make a track where you choose to walk.
Every action has a reaction.
No, you are not swallowed up
by the majesty of this breath-taking earth.
You share its beauty,
because of your living, breathing
part in it.

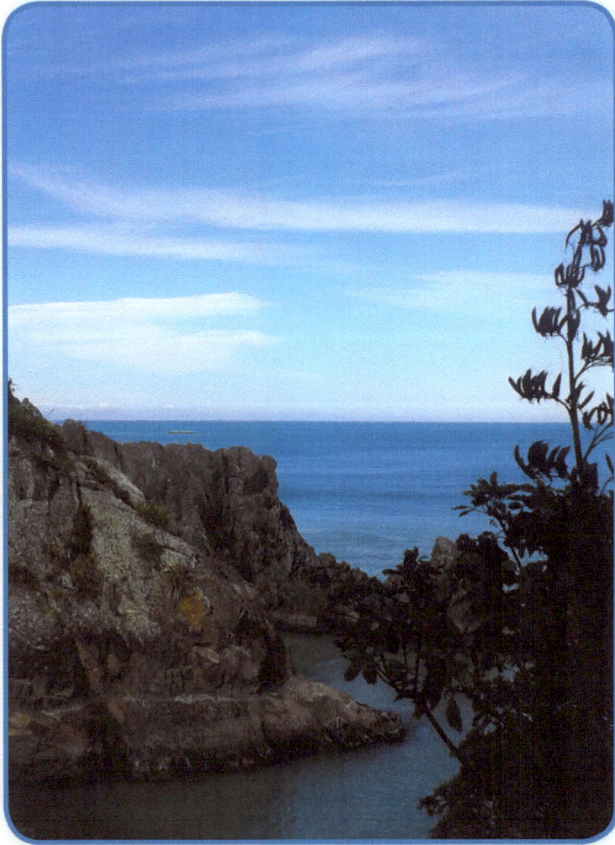

'Come, all you who are thirsty, come to the waters;
and you who have no money, come, buy and eat!
Come, buy wine and milk without money and without cost.
Why spend money on what is not bread,
and your labour on what does not satisfy?
Listen, listen to me, and eat what is good,
and you will delight in the richest of fare.
Give ear and come to me;
listen, that you may live...'

ISAIAH 55:1-3 (NIV)

Momentarily

For a moment,

I gaze at you.
And it's as though
the curtains of heaven are pulled aside
to let you through.
As though you bend
down to kiss my upheld brow,
so briefly, that I

mesmerized,

struggle to contain your presence,
and frame your memory.
And must keep searching,
all the length
of my days and nights,
for glimpses of you,
alive again,

in my sight.

While I know you are there
in reality,
it's just reality has a way
of colouring things grey.
As we live out our existence
in the rush of tomorrows expectations
and today's claims,

on our time.

But the light
still seeks me out,
rays of silver,
tracing patterns on the floor;
and if I take a moment
and turn and really open my eyes,
I see you, seeing me.

Living Light.

'For now we see only a reflection as in a mirror;
then we shall see face to face. Now I know in part;
then I shall know fully, even as I am fully known.'
1 CORINTHIANS 13:12 (NIV)

Mosaics

We are mosaics, you and I.
Each part designed.
Each piece patterned and coloured,
to blend in to the pieces beside.

We are mosaics, you and I.

All our strengths and flaws,
our light and our shade,
intricately designed.

To make a beautiful, perfect whole.

No we are not meant to hide,
those parts of which we're shy.
Or which we cannot perceive,
could serve any purpose at all.

For we cannot see the image of ourselves,
which others see revealed.
Yet God has made of us a storybook,
for those around us to read.

Our true purpose, to be real.

Yes, we are mosaics, you and I,
designed to hang in the light.
When all the colours and the patterns merge,
the picture meant is evident.

Mosaics, you and I.

Our beauty not easily defined, by this world.
As each person sees in us something different,
for which God has given them eyes.

Our gift, simply to be ourselves,
and reflect the artist's design.

'Now you are the body of Christ,
and each one of you is a part of it.'
1 CORINTHIANS 12:27 (NIV)

Together

How would it be if we all hung out our washing together
on the line?
What if we were brave enough to show the faded sheets
with the holes at the end,
the socks that still need darning,
the trousers with frayed hems?

What if we chose right now, to no longer pretend?
To the world, the neighbours, our friends.
If we could shout out, "I'm not good enough,
I'm hardly even close.
It's all pretense, and God only knows
the truth"?

What if we exchanged our truest selves,
like linen table coverings hanging in the sun?
Plain and laid bare,
with a spot here and there;
that we might normally cover,
with the table runner.

What if we chose not to disguise the flaws?
But let them hang out in the sun.
Whipping in the breeze, free and light.
No longer burdensome,
but at ease in the peace,
of lessened expectations.

What if we were kind?
Not just to others, but to ourselves.
What if we turned that smile inwards?
And the grace that we have learned to impart,
to other's failings,
we generously gave ourselves.

What if we were to say "I'm not good. I'm far from.
But I am trying, as hard as anyone, and that's enough"?
For saying that out loud, we might just find,
has a magic to absolve us
from the shame,
of all the things we keep inside.

Like washing in the light,
of the sun.

'Those who look to him are radiant;
their faces are never covered with shame.'
PSALM 34:5 (NIV)

Creator God

Creator God,
what inspiration you give,
to make, to create
things worthy of your benevolence.

Yes we know if we could store
all the blessings that you give,
then we could use those gifts
to bless an entire world.

But our minds and hearts are weak
at receiving fully from you,
and much that you would favour us with
we foolishly sieve through.

But we thank you God
that your gifts to us are limitless,
and what we do manage to retain
you increase for our benefit.

And for the good of others,
which in the end is your purpose.
That we would not hold on to
our blessings, but pour them out in gratitude.

Oh yes good God,
what inspiration you give,
when we take hold of your goodness;
to join with you in creating,

something far beyond us.

'*But ask the animals, and they will teach you,*
or the birds in the sky, and they will tell you;
or speak to the earth, and it will teach you,
or let the fish in the sea inform you.
Which of all these does not know
that the hand of the Lord has done this?
In his hand is the life of every creature
and the breath of all mankind.'
JOB 12:7-10 (NIV)

When Love Breaks In

I believe, it is

the wounded things that are
the most beautiful.

And that we break open to the light,
because nothing is meant to remain inside.

Sorrow is but a well of understanding.
Chaos but a path to new revelation.
Pain a pearl that shows us where it hurts,

so that the light may trace
the ache to its source.

I believe, it is

that the weak receive
the strength they truly need.

As dependence brings us
to a full and deep surrender.

Shame is but a robe we must discard.
Guilt, another's pain breaking our hearts.
Remorse, a path to redeem our tortured selves.

And as weakness girds our prayers with heavenly power,
the light reveals the darkness as a fraud.

And so I believe it is,
when love breaks in.

'...because of the tender mercy of our God,
by which the rising sun will come to us from heaven
to shine on those living in darkness
and in the shadow of death,
to guide our feet into the path of peace.'
LUKE 1:78-79 (NIV)

Live

God says 'blossom', to the bud
and it opens wide to drink in the sun.

God says 'grow' to the seedling
and it lifts its head to seek the light.

God says 'live' to the child
and it breathes its first empowering breath.

God indwells the wonders he creates.
The author and inhabiter of our frames.

We blossom, we grow and we live.
Because of his word inscribed within.

Our DNA, his intended plan,
to grace the world with a unique offering.

So blossom wide.
Grow to heights yet unimagined.

Dance to the music which sets you alight.
And laugh and live as God has ordained.

For there will never be a 'you' again,
and life…

Life is waiting.

'Though it is the smallest of all seeds,
yet when it grows, it is the largest of
garden plants and becomes a tree,
so that the birds come and perch in its branches.'
MATTHEW 13:32 (NIV)

The Gift

This day,
may love rise in your heart, as the sun.
May the gift of life
cause your own springs to fill.
As a river, with a source eternal.

Or as a tree, planted deep in the earth
draws from the richest nourishment.

This day,
may you know Mary's smile,
as you hold close
to your receptive heart, the new-born Christ,
the gift of a love indescribable;

and in awareness of the reason for his birth,
recall the value of his life to all mankind.

This day,
may the star you have followed,
lead you to fall in worship at his feet.
May you not miss the humble appearance,
of a love which seeks no entrance;

but in its tender innocence,
holds the whole world captive.

'Today in the town of David a Saviour has been born to you;
he is the Messiah, the Lord.'
LUKE 2:11 (NIV)

A Candle in the Darkness

I see the candle glow,
see it light the dark.
Flickers of light in the shadows,
I watch it dance.

I see how it glows and dims,
yet fails to go out.
Charged with energy at its core
it keeps itself alight.

I carry its flame,
to use to light another.
Before long the shadows become scarcer,
and the light in the room is doubled.

I sit in the warmth of their glow,
thinking how it didn't take much,
to keep the darkness at bay.
And so it is with the power of love.

*'Out of his fullness we have all received grace
in place of grace already given.'*
JOHN 1:16 (NIV)

Friendship

Friends that come easy,
easily go.

Friends that come slowly,
quietly grow.

Until friendship is a tree
with its roots deep entrenched,
and its years of growth etched,
on the rings of its trunk.

Friends who mean much,
are not just found.

Friends that matter,
are not here and gone.

No, they're made and kept,
by shared experience;
and strengthened by bonds,
that remain over time.

Love and affection,
loyalty and trust.

Admiration and regard,
hold them close to us.

Until they are honed like diamonds
to a lasting strength;
and impressed upon
the heart of us.

'A friend loves at all times, and a brother
is born for a time of adversity.'
PROVERBS 17:17 (NIV)

Grace

Grace

tender and gentle as the rain from heaven.
Drawing us
to a willing and yielding repentance,
surrendering all,
nothing withheld.

Until goodness becomes something worn then,
as an award,
giving us access to God's presence,
while all is well,
and our path easy to follow.

But when the struggle comes
and we find
we're flesh and blood.
Not so good as we thought at all,
rather bent on doing wrong,

then grace.

Tender and gentle, and wrapped in understanding,
we find, is also strong.
Strong as a parent's grip
with a reach that defies,
all our running.

Grace is the father who searches for us,
in our hearts
where we are blind
and lights up all the dark,
until there's no more hiding.

And we understand then, never to judge,
another's stumbling walk,
or to be too proud of our own.
For there is a time for us all,
when our deep need brings us to our knees.

And his great grace is beyond what we knew, or understood, before.
And we realise then, in our weakness, that only the unworthy receive.

'For it is by grace you have been saved, through faith.
And this is not from yourselves. It is a gift of God.'
EPHESIANS 2:8 (NIV)

Whole

There is something I've been trying to grasp.
A truth you would have me understand.
From these lessons, with no explanation,
I seek reasons for their being.
And think, there must be a plan,
or else, chaos.

And that is not how you work,
although we know it's from inside out.
And we know you make us fools,
despite our thinking we are right,
and you use us then, as broken tools,
meant to confound the wise.

Yes, I'm learning that in your upside-down world,
weak does not mean defective.
Nor does cracked mean I'm far from whole,
but simply that I haven't shattered;
and I'm actually stronger in my walk with you,
than I truly knew.

Yes, I read today that doubt is
not faith's opposite, as I thought,
rather it's an element of our journey to belief,
and precedes the faith that follows it.
If that is true, then I can trust my fears to you,
though all may appear, as lost.

And love, love is made stronger still,
for the strain on its roots.
And the desert, beyond all appearances,
can bloom as a rose, and springs burst forth
where it appeared there were no water, before.
And dry bones can be revived.

Yes, this is the something I have been trying to grasp.
In the chapel, upon the floor,
and in bed, with the width of miles, between opposing views,
I found you whisper it to me, loud and clear.
It's just I couldn't at first believe what you said,
that we could be 'broken and still whole'.

'But when he, the Spirit of truth, comes, he
will guide you into all the truth.
He will not speak on his own; he will speak only what he hears,
and he will tell you what is yet to come.'
JOHN 16:13 (NIV)

A New Year

The new year comes to us,
ready yet or not.
While we may prefer to burrow deep
into the old.

The new year comes,
with untold stories to unfold.
And dreams that might bear fruit,
if we're bold.

To open the door
to infinite possibility.
To recall
what a blank canvas can reveal.

What a pen, that meets an empty page,
can unveil.
What a life fully assured of its future,
can rightly claim.

Gold.
Like the sun rising, the new year comes.
Reminding us,
that life renews itself, like all things.

The old is gone,
until there is no ground upon which to hide.
And we burrow out like cicadas into the light.
And sing with newly opened eyes.

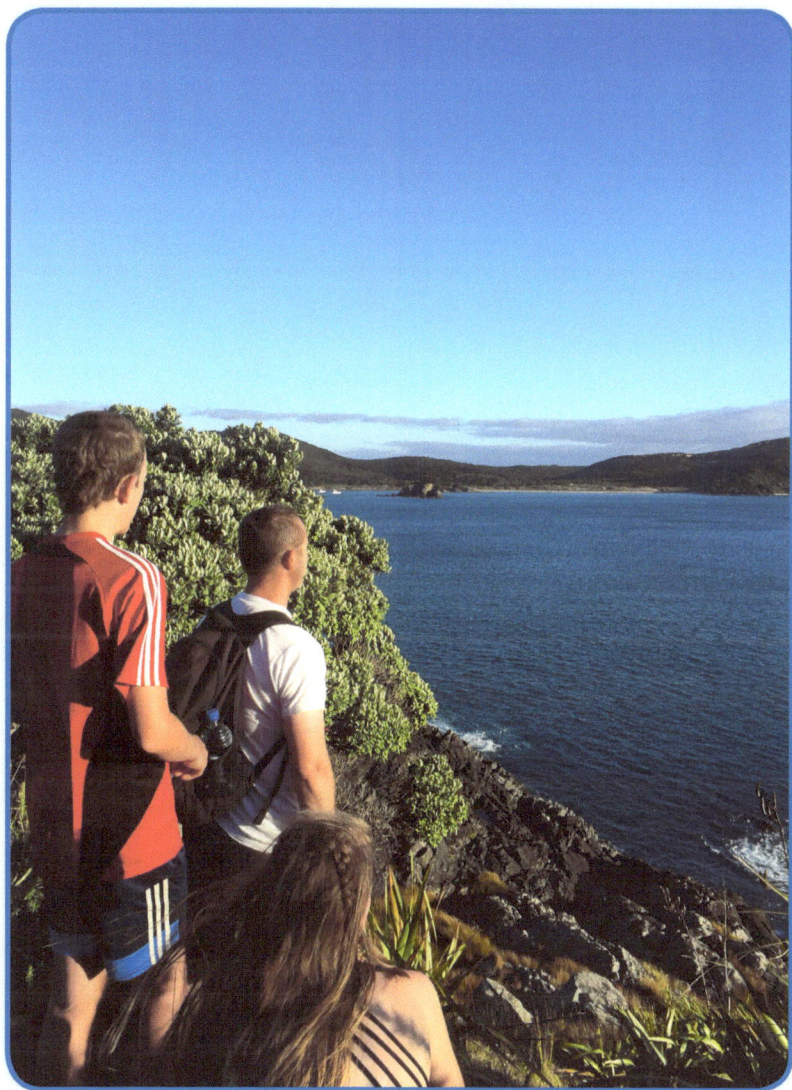

'In the morning I will sing of your love.'
PSALM 59:16 (NIV)

A Love Story

It's a love story.
As all good lovers know
there is a blueprint to follow,
for a love story
to ring true.

And your love for us
is the love of a lifetime,
an eternity even,
from the beginning,
of time, to amen.

Your love for us
exists in every note,
of all the lovers' ballads,
which man has ever yet
composed.

Oh yes, your love for us
lies woven in every story
ever told,
which spoke of daring,
and of loss,

and triumph after all.

Yes, your love for us
is in the hearts of everyone;
of all who love
wholeheartedly,
only to have to go on alone.

For your love, in truth
is lived out by us.
In all of us,
who behold your story,
and allow it to determine our part.

From the cradle
to the cross,
from time's beginning
to your sacrifice,
and its final accomplishment.

We wait, and we trust,
and we know just a little
of what it is to love
truly,
because you've shown us.

What it means to come and give up,
to lose what can't be kept,
to gain what can't be lost.

*'All those who have waited with love for him
to come again will receive a crown.'*
2 TIMOTHY 4:8 (NIV)

Twilight

In the soft twilight I stood, at the water's edge,
the river touched by the dying sun.
The world still, as though holding her breath,
while in the distance a lyric was sung.

A bird was fare-welling the day's last hour,
with a melody on the gentle breeze.
My heart responded, to the reverent prayer
resounding in the timeless hymn.

Across the water, the forest lay green,
resplendent in the magical light.
And above the depths a star was lit,
to herald the coming of the night.

With it came the wind in a gust that chilled.
My heart mourned for the moment gone.
The sun made her departure beyond the hills,
and I like the river made for home.

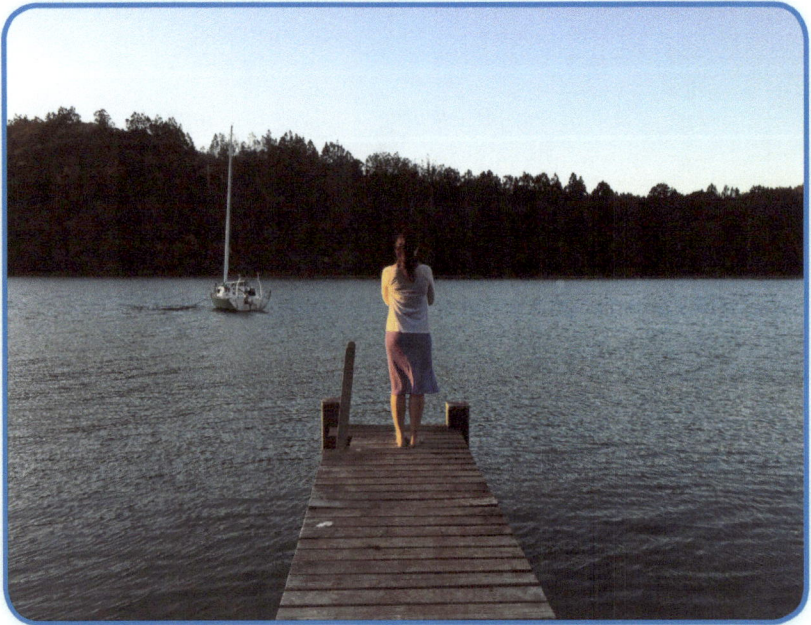

'Lord, our Lord, how majestic is your name in all the earth!'
PSALM 8:9 (NIV)

Let Me Rise

'Let me rise
in your heart.
Lay there and let me rise.
The door to the tomb is open.
The door to your heart.
Don't be afraid of the silence.
It's as silent as the tomb
on Easter morning.
Wide open.

'The sun shines on the place
where I lay.
The silence of Sunday morning,
only broken by bird song.
It's the silence that speaks
to your heart now.
Lay there and look at the sky.
The clouds that point the way,
to me.

'You now live in the place,
between the cross and
the resurrection.
But look closely.
The door has been opened,
to your heart.
And the Son shines in.
Follow the light to me.
I am the way.'

'But for you who revere my name,
the sun of righteousness will rise with healing in its rays.'
MALACHI 4:2 (NIV)

Photo Appendix

Cover: As Catedrais Beach, 'Beach of the Cathedrals', Lugo, Spain (By Lyn Chaffart, Editor Scriptural Nuggets (scripturalnuggets.org) and Author of 'Aboard God's Train – A Journey with God through the Valley of Cancer.' Used with permission.)

Words: Matai Bay, Karikari Peninsula, New Zealand

Walking Home: Matai Bay, Karikari Peninsula, New Zealand

Wait: Stanmore Bay, Whangaparaoa, New Zealand

The Silver Lining: Blenheim, Marlborough, New Zealand

Back: Matai Bay, Karikari Peninsula, New Zealand

Understanding: Little Oneroa Beach, Waiheke Island, Auckland, New Zealand

Fooling Ourselves: Piha Beach, Waitakere, Auckland, New Zealand

The Night Watchman: Blenheim, Marlborough, New Zealand

As with Love: Marlborough Sounds, New Zealand

An Ending: Rapaura Beach, Marlborough, New Zealand

Trust Him: Waitakere Ranges Forest Park, Auckland, New Zealand

Let Go: Bethalls Beach, Waitakere, Auckland, New Zealand

I Love: Stanmore Bay, Whangaparaoa, New Zealand.

Seal Me: Matai Bay, Karikari Peninsula, New Zealand

Self Compassion: Karangahake Gorge, Waihi, New Zealand

Silence: Matai Bay, Karikari Peninsula, New Zealand

Rest: Matai Bay, Karikari Peninsula, New Zealand

My Little Flower: Blenheim, Marlborough, New Zealand

Loved: Piha Beach, Waitakere, Auckland, New Zealand

Love is Not: Raglan, New Zealand

His Light: Mahurangi Regional Park, Mahurangi Peninsula, Auckland, New Zealand

Cocooned: Matai Bay, Karikari Peninsula, Auckland, New Zealand

Come: Rapaura Beach Headland, Marlborough, New Zealand

Momentarily: Matai Bay, Karikari Peninsula, Auckland, New Zealand

Mosaics: Picton, Marlborough Sounds, New Zealand

Together: Matai Bay, Karikari Peninsula, Auckland, New Zealand

Creator God: Whites Bay, Marlborough, New Zealand

When Love Breaks In: Mahurangi Regional Park, Mahurangi Peninsula, Auckland, New Zealand

Live: Little Oneroa Beach, Waiheke Island, New Zealand

The Gift: Matai Bay, Karikari Peninsula, New Zealand

A Candle in the Darkness: Piha Beach, Waitakere, Auckland, New Zealand

Friendship: Piha Beach, Waitakere, Auckland, New Zealand

Grace: Raglan, New Zealand

Whole: Piha Beach, Waitakere, Auckland, New Zealand

A New Year: Matai Bay, Karikari Peninsula, New Zealand

A Love Story: Karikari Peninsula, New Zealand

Twilight: Okura River, Okura, Auckland, New Zealand

Let me Rise: Karikari Peninsula, New Zealand

www.ingramcontent.com/pod-product-compliance
Lightning Source LLC
Chambersburg PA
CBHW051233090426
42740CB00001B/1